Promises For A Woman of *Purpose*

Embracing God's Promises for You as a Woman of Purpose

Devotional and Journal

This Journal Belongs to:

_____

DEDICATION

I wish to dedicate this journal to every woman who is discovering or has discovered their life purpose. Be authentically you, live in alignment with who you came here to become, unapologetically.

Promises For A Woman of *Purpose*

Embracing God's Promises for You as a Woman of Purpose
Devotional and Journal

Welcome to Your Purpose

As a lover of God, wife, mother, author, entrepreneur, speaker and teacher, I did not always know what my purpose was. I have experienced as a child, domestic violence, insecurities, family issues, guilt, shame, fear, unloved, worthless, anger, confusion, frustration, pressures as a teenager, identity crisis, domestic violence as a young woman, relationship issues, college, pressures of an adult, miscarriages, married three times, divorced twice, career issues, business owner failures as early as 18 years of age and so many other struggles and fear. However, once I moved out of my own way and God stepped in, I no longer had an identity crisis. I now have an identity revelation, walking by faith and not by sight into my purpose, ON PURPOSE!

The intent of this journal is to empower and remind you of your divine attributes, authority and God-given purpose, to be still and let go of your fears and struggles. Listen, I'll be the first to say that process is very uncomfortable but in the end, when it is all revealed, like opening a beautifully wrapped present, it will work out for your good.

As you take notes weekly, you will begin to find true meaning in your life to make a conscious shift in your life, purposefully.

*This journey is not easy, but it is one that we must continue to trod. Everything that you have been through WILL NOT be wasted! Celebrate every moment, every process. I invite you to avail yourself to the pages before you and maintain your journey through this journal.
Know that I love you!*

- Tschanna M. Taylor, MBA, CCLC, CRMC

Contents

Renewed Mind

The Struggle in Our Minds
Ephesians 4:23

Have you ever been in a setting where you compliment another woman on how beautiful she looks, only for her to say something negative about herself? I believe that God's heart breaks to see so many beautiful women He created not move past their own faux pas to recognize just how marvelous they really are. The comments we make negatively originate from the heart and sometimes, words unspoken do just as much damage. A woman's mind is the first line of defense against Satan's lies. If we can gain control of our thoughts, replacing negativity with God's truths, we will be free to recognize and acknowledge the beauty internally and externally. Spend time this week digging into God's Word and memorize scriptures that combat Satan's lies fed to you.

Affirmation: I have the mind of Christ.

Weekly Reflections

This week's scripture that I hold onto dearly is:

_____

A lesson that I am currently learning/have learned or that God is teaching me/has taught me this week is/was:

_____

_____

_____

_____

_____

Before the end of the week, I need to do:

My Mess Into a Masterpiece=My Purpose
Psalm 138:8

Much is written about purpose these days, because we all came here for a reason. What does God want you to do with your life? Apostle Paul was concerned about his purpose as well. He said that his desire was that he could take hold of that purpose for which Jesus had took hold of him (Phil. 3:12). Before Paul was a believer, He was on his way to Damascus to persecute Christians when God stopped him with a blinding light and introduced Paul to Jesus. Remember in my intro to this journal, I briefly shared my mess. God turned my mess into my masterpiece, on purpose. Although your conversion may not have been as drastic as Paul's, your being chosen as God's child is just as miraculous. Finding God's purpose is a challenge because God knows what that purpose is. Finding God's purpose is also a comfort because we don't have to fill someone else's shoes. His purpose for you is designed just for you. And He will reveal it one day at a time as you look to Him for guidance. If you haven't done so already, ask God to help you lay hold of your purpose for your life. Then get ready for the masterpiece to be created.

Affirmation: Each day I see my life's purpose more clearly.

Weekly Reflections

This week's scripture that I hold onto dearly is:

_____

A lesson that I am currently learning/have learned or that God is teaching me/has taught me this week is/was:

_____
_____
_____
_____

Before the end of the week, I need to do:

Forgiveness Can Be Tricky!
Colossians 3:13

God's Word teaches us that we're to forgive those who hurt us. When we invest our time and emotions into a relationship, allowing ourselves to trust and be vulnerable with others, there are bound to be times when we get hurt. We are imperfect and none of us are immune to hurting others or being hurt ourselves. The truth is, no matter how strong our friendship bonds are, without forgiveness every single one of our friendships would be short lived. Forgiveness can be tricky. This process isn't easy, but it works. Take a moment below and ask the Lord to open your eyes and heart to reveal anyone in your life that you have not completely forgiven.

Affirmation: *I live in the now and design my future. My past has no effect on my present.*
Weekly Reflections

This week's scripture that I hold onto dearly is:
_____

A lesson that I am currently learning/have learned or that God is teaching me/has taught me this week is/was:

_____

_____

_____

_____

_____

Before the end of the week, I need to do:

Subtle Deception
1 Peter 5:8

Dear God, I know that I am Your child and that You want me to life a life free from Satan's deceptions. Search my mind and reveal any areas of my thought life in which I have allowed Satan to gain a foothold. I want to be filled with joy and with Your Hold Spirit! In Jesus' name I ask these things. Amen.

Affirmation: I dedicate myself to personal transformation through the renewing of my mind.

Weekly Reflections

This week's scripture that I hold onto dearly is:

_____

A lesson that I am currently learning/have learned or that God is teaching me/has taught me this week is/was:

_____

_____

_____

_____

_____

Before the end of the week, I need to do:

Ephesians 6:11-13

Forgiveness

Once Broken, Now Mended
Philippians 4:8

Satan loves to trap us with subtle deception aimed at our minds, especially when our defenses are down. The first step to a renewed mind is recognizing his deceptions. The second step to a renewed mind is mending our thoughts-replacing Satan's lies with God's truth. This week, camp out in Philippians 4:4-9 and write out these scriptures in your own words as they apply to your circumstances right now.

Affirmation: I take responsibility for my thoughts.

Weekly Reflections

This week's scripture that I hold onto dearly is:

_____

A lesson that I am currently learning/have learned or that God is teaching me/has taught me this week is/was:

_____

_____

_____

_____

_____

Before the end of the week, I need to do:

This Baggage is Heavy
1 Corinthians 2:10-11

Our souls can never be completely mended until we let go of the heavy baggage (fear, hurt, shame, doubt, anger, abuse, neglect, etc.) and replace that weight with the light yoke of God's peace. It may seem impossible now, but when we understand what forgiveness is and what it is not, we will see that forgiveness is attainable. When you feel the familiar pangs of hurt from an offense you've already decided to forgive, cry out to the Lord, "Increase my faith!".

Affirmation: I am ready to be healed. I am willing to forgive. All is well.

Weekly Reflections

This week's scripture that I hold onto dearly is:

_____

A lesson that I am currently learning/have learned or that God is teaching me/has taught me this week is/was:

_____

_____

_____

_____

_____

Before the end of the week, I need to do:

Turning Over a New Leaf
Matthew 18:21-22

"Turning over a new leaf" means changing for the better. This also entails being forgiving. It takes courage to forgive-to give up resentment, anger, and hurt. Only the brave will forgive. Only the strong will have the courage to let go of the past. Forgiving doesn't say, "What you did was okay." No, the offense was wrong; however; if you do not forgive, you are the loser, continuing to carry a heavy backpack of trash from the past. And trash stinks! Paul instructs us, "Bear with each other and forgive one another if any of you has a grievance against someone. Forgive as the Lord forgave you" The Lord's unlimited forgiveness is our pattern to follow. With God's help, you will turn over a new leaf. List one thing that you know you should let go and surrender.

Affirmation: Through surrender, I move from outer turmoil to inner peace.

Weekly Reflections

This week's scripture that I hold onto dearly is:

_____

A lesson that I am currently learning/have learned or that God is teaching me/has taught me this week is/was:

_____

_____

_____

_____

_____

Before the end of the week, I need to do:

Prepared for Growth
Galatians 5:1

*Whether you've experienced abuse, bitterness, discouragement or fear, God sets us free in two ways: through forgiving us and by releasing us from the bondage of being a product of our past. We can either allow guilt and shame to trap our hearts or we can replace these debilitating emotions with godly sorrow. The latter serves as the catalyst for tremendous growth in our walk with God. Understanding who you are in Christ is the first step in letting go of the past. Once you understand who you are **now**, you can release yourself from who you were **then**. Write a letter from God to you, reminding you to let get and embrace your position in Him.*

(Ex: Dear _____,   Love God,)

Affirmation: I will let go of the past that I do not need and create the future that I want.

Weekly Reflections

This week's scripture that I hold onto dearly is:

_____

A lesson that I am currently learning/have learned or that God is teaching me/has taught me this week is/was:

_____

_____

_____

_____

_____

Before the end of the week, I need to do:

Ephesians 4:31-32

Healing

Refreshing Words from Psalms
Psalm 8

Lord, our Lord, how majestic is your name in all the earth! When I consider your heavens, the work of your fingers, the moon and stars, which you have set in place, what is mankind that you are mindful of them, human beings that you care for them? You have made them a little lower than the angels and crowned them with glory and honor. You made them rulers over the works of your hands; you put everything under their feet; Lord, our Lord, how majestic is your name in all the earth!

I feel insignificant today, Lord. Thank you for your greatness- and Your care for me!

Affirmation: I trust that everything will be restored back to me in His perfect timing.

Weekly Reflections

This week's scripture that I hold onto dearly is:

_____

A lesson that I am currently learning/have learned or that God is teaching me/has taught me this week is/was:

_____
_____
_____
_____

_____

Before the end of the week, I need to do:

A Reason to Dance, He's Lifted My Sorrows
Psalm 30:11-12

Gospel artist Ron Kenoly sings the song, Mourning into Dancing and God has done this in my life on numerous occasions and every time I think about it, I get excited because God is truly a healer. In every process we face, you may or may not feel completely restored and that's okay. But as you continue to apply God's principles to your life, He will faithfully complete the work. Just thinking about the hope you have in Christ should be enough to start your feet dancing. Dance like David danced and document your journey below.

Affirmation: I am healed!

Weekly Reflections

This week's scripture that I hold onto dearly is:

_____

A lesson that I am currently learning/have learned or that God is teaching me/has taught me this week is/was:

_____

_____

_____

_____

_____

Before the end of the week, I need to do:

I Need a Healing for My Soul
Isaiah 43:18

Memories...It can be a tremendous blessing as we recall happy moments from the past. But memories can also be tremendously painful. I remember a time when I was a member of an organization where I gave it my all but I was hurt from the belittlement and untruths that were displayed, which no longer served, for values that were near to my heart. Because of this, I felt that most organizations such as this were all the same but I had to change my thoughts and turn it all over to Jesus. It's time to erase the memories of the past and not make this to be a monument in your mind. Every time a painful memory comes to your mind, bring it to God. Today is the only day that we have, Yesterday is gone, and whether we have a tomorrow is unknown. Leave it with God. He can give you a healing for your soul.

Affirmation: I choose healing for my heart, mind, body and spirit.

Weekly Reflections

This week's scripture that I hold onto dearly is:

_____

A lesson that I am currently learning/have learned or that God is teaching me/has taught me this week is/was:

_____

_____

_____

_____

_____

Before the end of the week, I need to do:

Stuck In Pain
Ephesians 4:23

Is your life a bed of roses. Free from problems? I know my life isn't. I've noticed through my own painful experiences that sometimes we get stuck in our pain. When I am stuck in my pain, no one else is responsible for my feelings except for me. I may not be able to change the circumstances, but I can choose my attitude toward them. The ultimate source of your total healing comes from the Lord. If your faith is weak, tell God. He'll help you to get unstuck.

Affirmation: I release all of my old pain.

Weekly Reflections

This week's scripture that I hold onto dearly is:

_____

A lesson that I am currently learning/have learned or that God is teaching me/has taught me this week is/was:

_____
_____
_____
_____
_____

Before the end of the week, I need to do:

1 Peter 5:10

Boldness

Possible, I'm Possible or I AM POSSIBLE
Luke 18:1-8

Those difficult moments you're dealing with right now- how do you see them? As insurmountable? Or as an opportunity for God to do the impossible? It's amazing what a difference attitude makes. Let's be clear. There is a possibility in those moments. Your challenges are golden opportunities for success. Right now when you pray about that overwhelming situation you're facing, don't worry that you're asking for too much. Pray big prayers because we have a big God-one who truly does the impossible, which encourages me that I AM POSSIBLE!

Affirmation: I am confident, bold and courageous. I AM POSSIBLE!

Weekly Reflections

This week's scripture that I hold onto dearly is:

_____

A lesson that I am currently learning/have learned or that God is teaching me/has taught me this week is/was:

_____

_____

_____

_____

_____

Before the end of the week, I need to do:

Bold as a Lion
Ephesians 3:12

You are braver than you know. You have the power within you to change the world. Being bold as a lion is doing things even when you're scared. Being brave isn't something that happens when you're not scared anymore. Brave people hear the whispers of fear but immediately take action to block it out. I remember the first time I spoke to the Women's Dept at my former church on Soul Ties. To see the women staring at me waiting for information on how to get free in their lives had me feeling nervous inside. My heart began to race. This type of conversation took courage anyway, right. But I knew that I had a purpose of being there and needed to push past my fears and deliver. This is why I can tell you, go be bold as a lion. Our purpose equips us to be who we've been called to be. Be brave. What is it that God has called you to but you've been too afraid to do it? Write your answer in the spaces below.

Affirmation: *I am fervent, bold, enthusiastic filled with joy.*

Weekly Reflections

This week's scripture that I hold onto dearly is:

_____

A lesson that I am currently learning/have learned or that God is teaching me/has taught me this week is/was:

_____
_____
_____
_____
_____

Before the end of the week, I need to do:

Setting the Stage
1 John 5:14

I'm sure if you're anything like me, you've read the story of Esther many times. Her authority, boldness, courage, and persistence is what stands out the most. She showed us that we can ask God for anything in HIS name. He tells us to be courageous and bold at all times, never to be afraid or worry. Set the stage by standing firm knowing that we must be courageous and bold, even when it is not popular to do so, and risk it all. Besides, the strongest source of courage in the face of fear is faith. Esther did exactly that in her journey of "setting the stage".

Affirmation: I am setting the stage.

Weekly Reflections

This week's scripture that I hold onto dearly is:

_____

A lesson that I am currently learning/have learned or that God is teaching me/has taught me this week is/was:

_____

_____

_____

_____

_____

Before the end of the week, I need to do:

Alone and Scared!
Deuteronomy 31:6

I remember when I was in my process of understanding why my husband sought attention from another woman. I went through all sorts of emotions during this time. I felt confused, angry, alone and scared. It was a lot of faith, prayer, fasting and meditation that brought me through the process. Let your faith in God give you the strength and courage to get through the difficult times. You must never forget that God is with you ALWAYS, even when you are alone and scared.

Affirmation: I am never alone!

Weekly Reflections

This week's scripture that I hold onto dearly is:

_____

A lesson that I am currently learning/have learned or that God is teaching me/has taught me this week is/was:

_____

_____

_____

_____

_____

Before the end of the week, I need to do:

Be
STRONG
and have
COURAGE
Do NOT be
AFRAID

Tschanna
TAYLOR

Joshua 1: 9

Vision

No Vision, You Perish!
Proverbs 29:18

Proverbs 29:18 state "Without a vision the people perish". Vision Is not getting together with a group of friends to cut out pretty pictures, words, and sayings on a poster board. Visions are necessary for life. My vision is what drives me to knowing instinctly that God has a better plan for me (Jeremiah 29:11 is my favorite scripture). I work a 9 to 5 that I view as my investor, I am stuck in rush hour traffic, taking me 2 hours to get home (Yep it's insane and nauseating only to have to repeat these steps Monday through Friday. I refuse to settle! Maybe it's not so easy, but when you acknowledge a vision that is your own, be prepared to begin one of the most rewarding experiences of your life. DO NOT ALLOW fear to block this process. Moses stuttered and was afraid to speak but God used him to lead his nation to freedom. What is your vision? Ask God to ignite in you a vision of the life HE wants you to live because without a vision, you perish.

Affirmation: I am worthy of all the best life has to offer me.

Weekly Reflections

This week's scripture that I hold onto dearly is:

_____

A lesson that I am currently learning/have learned or that God is teaching me/has taught me this week is/was:

_____
_____
_____
_____
_____

Before the end of the week, I need to do:

Don't Get Caught Up!
Amos 3:7

Fear isn't the only reason that dreams go unfulfilled. People get caught up in habits and living in secure routines. We sometimes get caught up in the everyday life of work, family, spouses, children, home, taxes, bills needing to be paid, church, vacation and more that we end up trapped serving routines that come with these responsibilities. And then there are the internal mental drivers at work. How about you? Do you have a feeling in the pit of your stomach that your life could be more? Do you have a desire to change your life or the life of others for the better? Maybe you've settled into a decent, but unfulfilling routine. Maybe you have robbed yourself of your dreams. Realizing this is a good starting point. Don't get caught up. Work your vision. .

Affirmation: I am receiving abundance now in expected and unexpected ways.

Weekly Reflections

This week's scripture that I hold onto dearly is:

_____

A lesson that I am currently learning/have learned or that God is teaching me/has taught me this week is/was:

_____

_____

_____

_____

_____

Before the end of the week, I need to do:

There Is More, Do You Believe It?
Proverbs 3:5-6

I remember when I received my Christian Life Coaching Certification in 2013. I was so excited to create my very first coaching program and in this rush of excitement also came fear, all rolled into this mix with clients waiting in the background. As I got more and more into my zone, there were some days that I really wanted to throw in the towel but God reminded me that I wasn't trusting in Him and stopped believing in the vision that He gave me. .I cried hysterically and thanked God for the reminder. When you step into your God-given purpose, there will be no doubt about it. Do you ever feel like you stopped believing in what God has called for you to do? If so, remember that you will have moments where you are nervous because you are stepping outside of your comfort zone; however, God has given you the grace to do it. Whatever you do, don't stop believing that there is more for you.

Affirmation: I am willing to believe that I am the creator of my life experience.

Weekly Reflections

This week's scripture that I hold onto dearly is:

_____

A lesson that I am currently learning/have learned or that God is teaching me/has taught me this week is/was:

_____

_____

_____

_____

_____

Before the end of the week, I need to do:

Vision Blockers
Ephesians 5:20

There is an African prover that says "Each of us is a seed of divinely inspired possibility, which when nurtured in its proper context can and will grow into the fullest expression of all we are supposed to become. Has God given you a vision that has yet to be manifested? Not sure where to begin? Is something keeping you from moving forward? In order to all that you can become, you must make an uncommon commitment to push through fear, doubt, not being clear on your goals, poor time management, lack of motivation, negative comments and procrastination just to name a few. You can push through these with the strength of the Lord. You can overcome these if you continue to press.

Affirmation: I have the power to create my own reality.

Weekly Reflections

This week's scripture that I hold onto dearly is:

_____

A lesson that I am currently learning/have learned or that God is teaching me/has taught me this week is/was:

_____

_____

_____

_____

_____

Before the end of the week, I need to do:

Habakkuk 2:2-3

Fearfully & Wonderfully Made

Who Am I?
Exodus 3:11

Sadly, the world we live in glamorizes perfection by telling lies through tv and social media that we are too thin, too fat, our hair is too short or not long enough and so on but if stop what you're doing, go walk over to the mirror and tell yourself, "I'm fearfully and wonderfully made" No doubt! Moses had this trouble too when the bush was on fire and God told him to lead the Israelites out of slavery in Egypt to the promised land, but Moses had doubts about who he was. Moses asked God, Who Am I and God told Moses, His name is I AM. Is there something that God is speaking to your heart about that He wants you to do? .When you have an assignment, what matters most is now who you are, but who God is, the majestic and mighty one who is with you ALWAYS.

Affirmation: God sees the good in me. I am grateful to be me.

Weekly Reflections

This week's scripture that I hold onto dearly is:

_____

A lesson that I am currently learning/have learned or that God is teaching me/has taught me this week is/was:

_____

_____

_____

_____

_____

Before the end of the week, I need to do:

Who's Really Concerned?
Psalm 23:1

Are you in a time where you feel down about something? Struggling just to keep your head above water? People when you need them most, may not always be there and that's ok, because God is concerned about you. The same way the Israelites were stuck under the tyranny of Pharaoh and God intervened, is the same way he is concerned about you. (Exodus 3:7-8) He hears you, He sees you, He will rescue you because He is concerned about you. He wants you to cast your care on Him.

Affirmation: With God, I am considered to be a treasure. I am valuable.

Weekly Reflections

This week's scripture that I hold onto dearly is:

_____

A lesson that I am currently learning/have learned or that God is teaching me/has taught me this week is/was:

_____

_____

_____

_____

_____

Before the end of the week, I need to do:

Who Are You Created to Be
Psalm 139:13-14

Psalm 139 is a beautiful picture of God's great care in creating each one of us. List five words to describe yourself besides being God's daughter. Write a short statement that explains who you are as a woman. Do you agree with what you written. Explain.

_____

_____

_____

Affirmation: Just as I am-I am loved!

Weekly Reflections

This week's scripture that I hold onto dearly is:

_____

A lesson that I am currently learning/have learned or that God is teaching me/has taught me this week is/was:

_____

_____

_____

_____

Before the end of the week, I need to do:

I Am God's Workmanship
Colossians 3:13

The Master Artist who sculpted the universe spared nothing in the creation of you, HIS workmanship. There is tremendous hope and freedom in truly believing and embracing God's view of you.

Affirmation: I live in the now and design my future. My past has no effect on my present.

Weekly Reflections

This week's scripture that I hold onto dearly is:

_____

A lesson that I am currently learning/have learned or that God is teaching me/has taught me this week is/was:

_____
_____
_____
_____
_____

Before the end of the week, I need to do:

I AM FEARFULLY AND WONDERFULLY MADE

Hope

Yet, I Will Rejoice!
Habakkuk 3:17-18

Read the above scripture, Write out your own paraphrase of the last verses of this book. Substitute your problem's for Habakkuk's. When you get to the part where Habakkuk says he will still be joyful and rejoice in the Lord in spite of all his problems, tell God yours and rejoice.

Affirmation: Hope is now, not later.

Weekly Reflections

This week's scripture that I hold onto dearly is:

_____

A lesson that I am currently learning/have learned or that God is teaching me/has taught me this week is/was:

_____
_____
_____
_____
_____

Before the end of the week, I need to do:

Hope Belongs to You
Psalm 31:24

Are you struggling to find hope in light of a dire situation? Find your true sustenance in the will and Word of God.

Affirmation: My victory is not dependent on circumstances, I overcome all trials.

Weekly Reflections

This week's scripture that I hold onto dearly is:

_____

A lesson that I am currently learning/have learned or that God is teaching me/has taught me this week is/was:

_____

_____

_____

_____

_____

Before the end of the week, I need to do:

Having Things Our Way
Colossians 3:13

Every woman struggles with different frustrations, depending on her personality, life stage, living situation, etc. Take a moment to assess what frustrations you face and how you can demonstrate patience, gentleness, and submission through those circumstances. Besides, this is not Burger King, Have it Your Way.

Affirmation: I will not allow negative circumstances to dictate my future.

Weekly Reflections

This week's scripture that I hold onto dearly is:

_____

A lesson that I am currently learning/have learned or that God is teaching me/has taught me this week is/was:

_____

_____

_____

_____

_____

Before the end of the week, I need to do:

Cultivate Joy
Psalm 32:11

God has given us so many reasons to celebrate. He doesn't waste the difficult times in our lives but uses them to develop HIS character in you. Want more joy, cultivate it!

Affirmation: *Joy is abundant all around me.*

Weekly Reflections

This week's scripture that I hold onto dearly is:

_____

A lesson that I am currently learning/have learned or that God is teaching me/has taught me this week is/was:

_____

_____

_____

_____

_____

Before the end of the week, I need to do:

Wisdom
Knowledge
Understanding

Ask!
Matthew 7:7

Ask! Sounds easy right? But for some, it's hard to do. God told us if anyone lacks wisdom they should ask for it by faith, without doubting. Just ask.

Affirmation: *God gave me the discernment to make sound decisions.*

Weekly Reflections

This week's scripture that I hold onto dearly is:

_____

A lesson that I am currently learning/have learned or that God is teaching me/has taught me this week is/was:

_____

_____

_____

_____

_____

Before the end of the week, I need to do:

Seize the Moment
Proverbs 3:13

Sometimes we think wisdom comes from the big moments but sometimes wisdom shines on us at the smallest times of faithfulness. Stay humble and seize the moment.

Affirmation: I have wisdom to seize the moment when presented to me.

Weekly Reflections

This week's scripture that I hold onto dearly is:

_____

A lesson that I am currently learning/have learned or that God is teaching me/has taught me this week is/was:

_____

_____

_____

_____

_____

Before the end of the week, I need to do:

The Power of Words
Psalm 119

I have hidden your words in my heart that I might not sin against you, Open my eyes that I may see wonderful things in your law. Your statues are my delight; they are my counselors. My soul is weary with sorrow; strengthen me according to your word. Your word, Lord, is eternal; it stands firm in the heavens. Your word is a lamp for my feet, a light on my path. Great peace have those who love your law, and nothing can make them stumble.

Lord help me to realize that Your Word is not like any other written word. Teach me how to love it and not neglect it.

Affirmation: At every opportunity, I expand my knowledge and understanding.

Weekly Reflections

This week's scripture that I hold onto dearly is:

_____

A lesson that I am currently learning/have learned or that God is teaching me/has taught me this week is/was:

_____
_____
_____
_____
_____

Before the end of the week, I need to do:

Wisdom is calling you, Will you answer?
Proverbs 3:20-23

Wisdom is calling out to those who she cares so much about. Do not allow circumstances pressure you into making wrong choices. Do not let the lines between right and wrong cause you to be blurry in your daily walk. Wisdom is calling you, Will you answer? .

Affirmation: I attract love, wealth and wisdom.

Weekly Reflections

This week's scripture that I hold onto dearly is:
_____

A lesson that I am currently learning/have learned or that God is teaching me/has taught me this week is/was:

_____
_____
_____
_____
_____

Before the end of the week, I need to do:

True
beauty
begins
inside.

Proverbs 31:30

Be Encouraged

Facing Life's Challenges
2 Chronicles 20:12

Whatever challenges we face In life, we have a choice; to either turn to God and bow down before Him or run away in fear. We will experience peaks and valleys but what is the strategy to overcome the challenge? If we cave in, we will be running for the rest of our lives. We are called for a purpose. Always believe that you have the victory.

Affirmation: I am a fighter and I never give up.

Weekly Reflections

This week's scripture that I hold onto dearly is:
_____

A lesson that I am currently learning/have learned or that God is teaching me/has taught me this week is/was:

_____

_____

_____

_____

_____

Before the end of the week, I need to do:

Prayer is a top priority!
1 Thessalonians 5:17

Pray about everything. God is there, ready to help. Communicate with Him throughout your day. This is how you experience intimate fellowship that enables us to face whatever life throws at us. Make a total commitment that prayer is our top priority throughout the day.

Affirmation: I am free from worry. I am well, safe and have peace.

Weekly Reflections

This week's scripture that I hold onto dearly is:
_____

A lesson that I am currently learning/have learned or that God is teaching me/has taught me this week is/was:

_____
_____
_____
_____
_____

Before the end of the week, I need to do:

My Way of Escape
1 Corinthians 10:13

When we are tempted, we may feel like trouble is on the way. We can trust God in these moments to know that he will provide a way of escape to resist your trial.

Affirmation:

Weekly Reflections

This week's scripture that I hold onto dearly is:

_____

A lesson that I am currently learning/have learned or that God is teaching me/has taught me this week is/was:

_____

_____

_____

_____

_____

Before the end of the week, I need to do:

When we trust Him completely, we can live out our God-given purpose freely!
Job 42:2

God's purpose for your life is so that you feel HIS presence, receive HIS power, and proclaim HIS name in victory.

Affirmation:

Weekly Reflections

This week's scripture that I hold onto dearly is:

_____

A lesson that I am currently learning/have learned or that God is teaching me/has taught me this week is/was:

_____
_____
_____
_____
_____

Before the end of the week, I need to do:

Tschanna Taylor

Purpose

The Lord will work out his plans for my life- for your loving kindness, Lord, continues forever. Don't abandon me-for you made me.

Psalms 138:8

God has selected you, so you must allow Him to direct and develop you.

Affirmation:

Weekly Reflections

This week's scripture that I hold onto dearly is:

_____

A lesson that I am currently learning/have learned or that God is teaching me/has taught me this week is/was:

_____

_____

_____

_____

_____

Before the end of the week, I need to do:

Ask, and you will be given what you ask for. Seek, and you will find. Knock and the door will be opened.
Matthew 7:7

Not only expect great things from God but attempt great things for God.

Affirmation:

Weekly Reflections

This week's scripture that I hold onto dearly is:
_____

A lesson that I am currently learning/have learned or that God is teaching me/has taught me this week is/was:

_____
_____
_____
_____
_____

Before the end of the week, I need to do:

Therefore, do not worry about tomorrow, for tomorrow will worry about itself. Each day has enough trouble of its own.
Matthew 6:34

God has a purpose for your pain and struggles. Always turn to Him in times of trouble. .

Affirmation:
Weekly Reflections

This week's scripture that I hold onto dearly is:

_____

A lesson that I am currently learning/have learned or that God is
teaching me/has taught me this week is/was:

_____

_____

_____

_____

_____

Before the end of the week, I need to do:

I knew you before you were formed within your mother's womb; before you were born I sanctified you and appointed you as my spokesman to the world.

Jeremiah 1:5

No matter at what age or stage of life, God is not concerned with your ability, but only with your availability to be used by Him.

Affirmation:

Weekly Reflections

This week's scripture that I hold onto dearly is:

_____

A lesson that I am currently learning/have learned or that God is teaching me/has taught me this week is/was:

_____

_____

_____

_____

Before the end of the week, I need to do:

Week-at-a-Glance Things To-Do List

Day of the Week: _____	Day of the Week: _____
☐ _____	☐ _____
☐ _____	☐ _____
☐ _____	☐ _____
☐ _____	☐ _____
☐ _____	☐ _____
☐ _____	☐ _____
☐ Exercise	☐ Exercise
☐ Have Fun	☐ Have Fun
☐ Daily Journal	☐ Daily Journal
☐ Drink Water	☐ Drink Water

Day of the Week: _____	Day of the Week: _____
☐ _____	☐ _____
☐ _____	☐ _____
☐ _____	☐ _____
☐ _____	☐ _____
☐ _____	☐ _____
☐ _____	☐ _____
☐ Exercise	☐ Exercise
☐ Have Fun	☐ Have Fun
☐ Daily Journal	☐ Daily Journal
☐ Drink Water	☐ Drink Water

Week-at-a-Glance Things To-Do List

Day of the Week: _____	Day of the Week: _____
☐ _____	☐ _____
☐ _____	☐ _____
☐ _____	☐ _____
☐ _____	☐ _____
☐ _____	☐ _____
☐ _____	☐ _____
☐ Exercise	☐ Exercise
☐ Have Fun	☐ Have Fun
☐ Daily Journal	☐ Daily Journal
☐ Drink Water	☐ Drink Water

Week-at-a-Glance Things To-Do List

Day of the Week: _____	Day of the Week: _____
☐ _____	☐ _____
☐ _____	☐ _____
☐ _____	☐ _____
☐ _____	☐ _____
☐ _____	☐ _____
☐ _____	☐ _____
☐ Exercise	☐ Exercise
☐ Have Fun	☐ Have Fun
☐ Daily Journal	☐ Daily Journal
☐ Drink Water	☐ Drink Water

Day of the Week: _____	Day of the Week: _____
☐ _____	☐ _____
☐ _____	☐ _____
☐ _____	☐ _____
☐ _____	☐ _____
☐ _____	☐ _____
☐ _____	☐ _____
☐ Exercise	☐ Exercise
☐ Have Fun	☐ Have Fun
☐ Daily Journal	☐ Daily Journal
☐ Drink Water	☐ Drink Water

Week-at-a-Glance Things To-Do List

Day of the Week: _____	Day of the Week: _____
☐ _____	☐ _____
☐ _____	☐ _____
☐ _____	☐ _____
☐ _____	☐ _____
☐ _____	☐ _____
☐ _____	☐ _____
☐ Exercise	☐ Exercise
☐ Have Fun	☐ Have Fun
☐ Daily Journal	☐ Daily Journal
☐ Drink Water	☐ Drink Water

Day of the Week: _____	Day of the Week: _____
☐ _____	☐ _____
☐ _____	☐ _____
☐ _____	☐ _____
☐ _____	☐ _____
☐ _____	☐ _____
☐ _____	☐ _____
☐ Exercise	☐ Exercise
☐ Have Fun	☐ Have Fun
☐ Daily Journal	☐ Daily Journal
☐ Drink Water	☐ Drink Water

Day of the Week: _____	Day of the Week: _____
☐ _____	☐ _____
☐ _____	☐ _____
☐ _____	☐ _____
☐ _____	☐ _____
☐ _____	☐ _____
☐ _____	☐ _____
☐ Exercise	☐ Exercise
☐ Have Fun	☐ Have Fun
☐ Daily Journal	☐ Daily Journal
☐ Drink Water	☐ Drink Water

Week-at-a-Glance Things To-Do List

Day of the Week: _____	Day of the Week: _____
☐ _____	☐ _____
☐ _____	☐ _____
☐ _____	☐ _____
☐ _____	☐ _____
☐ _____	☐ _____
☐ _____	☐ _____
☐ Exercise	☐ Exercise
☐ Have Fun	☐ Have Fun
☐ Daily Journal	☐ Daily Journal
☐ Drink Water	☐ Drink Water

Day of the Week: _____	Day of the Week: _____
☐ _____	☐ _____
☐ _____	☐ _____
☐ _____	☐ _____
☐ _____	☐ _____
☐ _____	☐ _____
☐ _____	☐ _____
☐ Exercise	☐ Exercise
☐ Have Fun	☐ Have Fun
☐ Daily Journal	☐ Daily Journal
☐ Drink Water	☐ Drink Water

Purposeful Reflective Questions

Sometimes getting the right answers is about asking the right questions. I hope these basic questions spur you to examine what you really want out of life, while fulfilling your God-given purpose. Only then can you live intentionally to have the business, family, and spiritual life you desire. Write in your journal if you find you need additional space

Goals & Dreams

What is the # 1 goal that you would like to accomplish in the next 30 days?

_____

_____

My life would be radically different if this one thing happened over the next 12 months.

_____

_____

This one obstacle is holding me back from pursuing my dreams.

_____

_____

For me to accomplish my goals, I need to stop doing this?

_____

_____

Describe to top two dreams of your personal life:

_____

_____

Faith

Do I consider myself a person of faith? If yes, what does being a person of faith mean to you?

_____

_____

This one thing distracts me from pursuing my faith, or any faith for that matter.

_____

_____

I'm committed to my faith
because..._____

_____

I've had distractions and failures in my life that block my ability to engage in my faith, they are

_____

_____

I understand that bitterness can stifle creativity, I need to apologize to the following people:

_____

_____

Family

Honestly, do you feel that your #1 priority is family?

_____

_____

If I only had one chance to teach my children this trait, it would be

_____

_____

Your children will eulogize you with one sentence. Finish this sentence. My mom/dad was

_____

_____

I want my personal legacy to be this

_____

_____

I would like to very much remove this one family dynamic

_____

_____

We only get one go through with our children. How are you showing them that they are important?

_____

_____

Career

If I woke up tomorrow with no limitations both geographically or financially, what would I do with the rest of my life?

_____

_____

Am I giving 110% to my current career? Why?

_____

_____

No question about it, I would leave my current career today if I could do this

_____

_____

I feel without question I'm directly in the center of what I'm called to do. Why?

_____

_____

Io excel in my current career, I need to do these two things sooner than later.

_____

_____

I want to accomplish this before the end of my career.

_____

_____

Finances

Right now today this is my greatest financial challenge

_____

_____

If I had the opportunity, I would make this long-term investment

_____

_____

I have two main reasons that I want to make more money. Here they are

_____

_____

This financial obligation has me sidetracked for years to come. I feel trapped

_____

_____

If I only had a few extra minutes a week, I would do this to improve my financial position, maybe a side hustle

_____

_____

What are your financial goals in the next 90 days

_____

_____

Relationships

If I could provide this one thing for my spouse, it would be amazing

_____

_____

If I could undo this one mistake and forget about it, I would

_____

_____

It may just be my personality, but I seem most understood about this topic

_____

_____

Someday I hope to have the chance to meet these two people

_____

_____

These two boundaries need to be implemented into my life to better protect my main relationships

_____

_____

There are givers and takers in relationships. I consider myself a

_____

_____

To better my relationship with my spouse, I need to start

_____

_____

Purpose Scriptures to Meditate On

Psalm 57:2   1 Peter 2:9   Acts 2:23   Acts 13:36   Colossians 1:16

Ecclesiastes 3:1   Jeremiah 29:11   Jeremiah 32:19   Job 42:2 Luke 7:30

Proverbs 16:4   Proverbs 19:21   Proverbs 20:5   Psalm 33:11

Psalm 138:8   Romans 8:28   Ephesians 2:10   Isaiah 46:10

Matthew 28:18-20   Psalm 16:11   Ephesians 3:20   John 10:10

Isaiah 53:10   Mark 8:31   Luke 18:37   2 Peter 2:3-8

2 Corinthians 8:21

Prayer Request

_____
_____
_____
_____
_____
_____
_____
_____
_____
_____
_____

Answered Prayer

_____
_____
_____
_____
_____
_____
_____
_____
_____
_____
_____
_____

Prayer Request

_____
_____
_____
_____
_____
_____
_____
_____
_____
_____

Answered Prayer

_____
_____
_____
_____
_____
_____
_____
_____
_____
_____

Prayer Request

_____
_____
_____
_____
_____
_____
_____
_____
_____
_____
_____

Answered Prayer

_____
_____
_____
_____
_____
_____
_____
_____
_____
_____
_____
_____

Prayer Request

_____
_____
_____
_____
_____
_____
_____
_____
_____
_____

Answered Prayer

_____
_____
_____
_____
_____
_____
_____
_____
_____
_____

Prayer Request

_____
_____
_____
_____
_____
_____
_____
_____
_____
_____

Answered Prayer

_____
_____
_____
_____
_____
_____
_____
_____
_____
_____
_____

Prayer Request

_____
_____
_____
_____
_____
_____
_____
_____
_____
_____

Answered Prayer

_____
_____
_____
_____
_____
_____
_____
_____
_____
_____
_____

Prayer Request

_____
_____
_____
_____
_____
_____
_____
_____
_____
_____
_____

Answered Prayer

_____
_____
_____
_____
_____
_____
_____
_____
_____
_____
_____

Prayer Request

_____
_____
_____
_____
_____
_____
_____
_____
_____
_____

Answered Prayer

_____
_____
_____
_____
_____
_____
_____
_____
_____
_____

Prayer Request

_____
_____
_____
_____
_____
_____
_____
_____
_____
_____
_____
_____

Answered Prayer

_____
_____
_____
_____
_____
_____
_____
_____
_____
_____
_____
_____

Prayer Request

_____
_____
_____
_____
_____
_____
_____
_____
_____
_____

Answered Prayer

_____
_____
_____
_____
_____
_____
_____
_____
_____
_____

Prayer Request

_____
_____
_____
_____
_____
_____
_____
_____
_____
_____
_____

Answered Prayer

_____
_____
_____
_____
_____
_____
_____
_____
_____
_____
_____

Prayer Request

_____
_____
_____
_____
_____
_____
_____
_____
_____
_____

Answered Prayer

_____
_____
_____
_____
_____
_____
_____
_____
_____
_____

Prayer Request

_____
_____
_____
_____
_____
_____
_____
_____
_____
_____
_____

Answered Prayer

_____
_____
_____
_____
_____
_____
_____
_____
_____
_____
_____

Prayer Request

_____
_____
_____
_____
_____
_____
_____
_____
_____
_____

Answered Prayer

_____
_____
_____
_____
_____
_____
_____
_____
_____
_____

Notes:

Notes:

Notes:

_____

_____

_____

_____

_____

_____

_____

_____

_____

_____

_____

_____

_____

_____

_____

_____

_____

_____

Notes:

Notes:

Notes:

Notes:

Notes:

We would like to hear from you!

Please share with us how this book has helped or blessed you. For additional needs, contact Tschanna Taylor at

Tschanna Taylor Enterprises
P.O. Box 73254 Durham, NC 27722 USA
or by email at info@tschannataylor.com.

Follow on social media @Tschanna Taylor

https://m.me/TschannaTaylor

Promises For A Woman of *Purpose*

Embracing God's Promises for You as a Woman of Purpose
Devotional and Journal